CRUISIN BALTIC SEA

Abbreviated Guide for Cruise Ship Passengers

Warnemünde & Berlin, Germany
Stockholm, Sweden
Tallin, Estonia
Helsinki, Finland
St. Petersburg, Russia
Copenhagen, Denmark

By Emile Baladi

Acknowledgment

This quick tourist guide book is the result of high condensation of the author's extensive knowledge of the Baltic's port of calls. This knowledge was obtained through many years of research and visits culminated with hundreds of lectures presented by the author on cruise ships plowing the Baltic Sea. Wikimedia and Google Earth Pro were two of other references utilized in the research and visual aids in this guide for which I am most appreciative and thankful.

Introduction

For over twelve years I conducted hundreds of lectures on cruise ships plowing all the five oceans of the world. At the end of each lecture, some of the passengers always asked me if they can purchase printed copies of the lecture. Most cruise ship passengers and other tourists are hungry for abbreviated information regarding the places they are going to visit. They will use the information to make their decision regarding what to see and which tour to take. The information should include what makes each tourist site important to visit. This publication integrates historical, geographical, meteorological and other applicable parameters regarding each recommended tourist site of the Baltic port of calls. It makes each reader well informed to prioritize and select the most economical method to tour/visit these sites.

Table of Contents

Acknowledgment... iii

Introduction iv

Warnemünde & Berlin, Germany.......................................1

Stockholm, Sweden (Venice of the North) 11

Tallinn, Estonia..21

St. Petersburg,...38

Russia...38

Helsinki, Finland..58

Copenhagen,..66

Denmark...66

Warnemünde & Berlin, Germany

Warnemünde: A seaside resort town is located on the Baltic Sea. Warnemünde is a district of the city of Rostock, 12 kilometers (one rail station stop) away. The town is the busiest cruise port in Germany. Most cruise ships plowing the Baltic Sea stop in Warnemünde.

The origin of the name: Mouth of the Warnow (Warnow river estuary).

Synopsis of History: Warnemunde was founded around 1200 AD. For several centuries remained as a small fishing village. By 1323 was purchased by the city of Rostock to guarantee its access to the Baltic. During the 19th century, Warnemunde started to develop as a sea resort. Warnemunde was part of East

Germany after World War II and until the unification with West Germany in 1990-1991.

Population: Approximately 8,800 inhabitants.

Geography: Located north northeast of Germany on the Baltic Sea.

Location of Warnemunde

Economy and Tourism: Warnemünde primary economy shifted from fishing to tourism. A cruise ship center was completed in 2005, a major contributor to the economy.

Currency: The Euro

Attractions: All the attractions listed below are within walking distance from the ship (See Warnemunde attractions map).

> **The lighthouse:** a 37 meter (121 feet), constructed in 1897, and still in use. From the tower, visitors can enjoy an excellent view of the Baltic Sea and the northern districts of Rostock.

The Lighthouse

The Warnemünder Planetenwanderweg: A 1:1 billionth scale model of the Solar System, with a 1.4-meter diameter sphere as a model of the Sun near the lighthouse. A true scaled distance of the planet in their orbits along a westward walking trail. The total scaled distance to the last planet is about 6 kilometer.

The old canal: Where fishing boats, several restaurants, hotels, and pubs are located.

The beaches: 3 kilometers of white sandy beaches, the widest on the German Baltic Sea.

The Church: a beautiful neogothic building, completed in 1866, on the western edge of the town.

The Church

Warnemünde's Attractions

Berlin: The capital of Germany is less than 2 hours (by bus or rail) from Warnemunde.

Points of interest in Berlin include the Berlin Wall, the Reichstag (Parliament), the Brandenburg Gate, Check Point Charlie, The Berlin Airlift Monument at Tempelhof, Gendarmenmarkt Square, Berlin Cathedral and various museums, such as The Pergamon Museum.

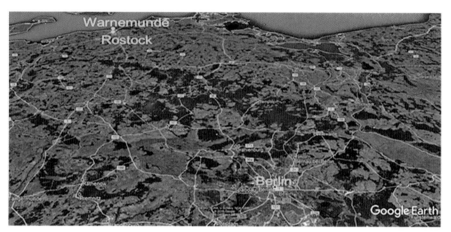

Map of northwest Germany

The Berlin Wall (Berlin)

The Reichstag (Berlin)

The Brandenburg Gate (Berlin)

Check Point Charlie (Berlin)

Berlin Airlift Monument (Berlin)

Gendarmenmarkt Square

Berlin Cathedral

The Pergamon Museum

Location of Point of Interest in Berlin

Climate Data for Warnemünde

Month	Jan	Feb	Mar	Apr	May	Jun	Jul	Aug	Sep	Oct	Nov	Dec
Ave. high °C (°F)	2.2 (36)	2.9 (37)	6.1 (43)	10.0 (50)	15.6 (60)	18.9 (66)	20.5 (69)	20.7 (69)	17.5 (64)	12.9 (55)	7.5 (46)	3.9 (39)
Daily mean °C (°F)	0.2 (32)	0.7 (33)	3.1 (38)	6.3 (43)	11.3 (52)	15.0 (59)	16.8 (62)	16.7 (62)	13.9 (57)	9.9 (50)	5.3 (42)	1.9 (35)
Ave. low °C (°F)	−1.9 (29)	−1.4 (30)	0.7 (33)	3.6 (39)	8.0 (46)	11.8 (53)	13.7 (57)	13.5 (56)	11.0 (52)	7.3 (45)	3.2 (38)	−0.1 (32)
Precip. mm (inches)	46 (1.8)	31 (1.2)	40 (1.6)	42 (1.7)	47 (1.9)	59 (2.3)	71 (2.9)	59 (2.3)	54 (2.1)	42 (1.7)	52 (2.1)	48 (1.9)

Climate Data for Berlin

Month	Jan	Feb	Mar	Apr	May	Jun	Jul	Aug	Sep	Oct	Nov	Dec
Rec. high °C (°F)	15.0 (59)	17.0 (63)	23.0 (73)	27.0 (81)	33.0 (91)	36.0 (97)	38.8 (102)	35.0 (95)	32.0 (90)	25.0 (77)	18.0 (64)	15.0 (59)
Ave. high °C (°F)	2.9 (37)	4.2 (40)	8.5 (47)	13.2 (56)	18.9 (66)	21.8 (71)	24.0 (75)	23.6 (75)	18.8 (66)	13.4 (56)	7.1 (45)	4.4 (40)
Ave. low °C (°F)	−1.5 (29)	−1.6 (29)	1.3 (34)	4.2 (40)	9.0 (48)	12.3 (54)	14.7 (59)	14.1 (57)	10.6 (51)	6.4 (44)	2.2 (36)	−0.4 (31)
Rec. low °C (°F)	−25 (−13)	−16 (3)	−13 (8)	−4 (25)	−1 (30)	4.0 (39)	7.0 (45)	7.0 (45)	0.0 (32)	−7 (19)	−9 (16)	−17 (1)
Precip. mm (inches)	42.3 (1.7)	33.3 (1.3)	40.5 (1.6)	37.1 (1.5)	53.8 (2.1)	68.7 (2.7)	55.5 (2.2)	58.2 (2.3)	45.1 (1.8)	37.3 (1.5)	43.6 (1.7)	55.3 (2.2)

Stockholm, Sweden (Venice of the North)

Stockholm: Consist of 1/3ʳᵈ water, 1/3ʳᵈ greenbelt & 1/3ʳᵈ city, giving Stockholm the freshest air of any European capital.

The name Stockholm: Stock means log (in old German means fortification) Holm means islet. Thus, Stockholm means fortified islet

Synopsis of History:

The Founding: 1252 AD The earliest mention of Stockholm. Founded by Burger Jarl* to protect Sweden from a sea invasion.

> ***Burger jarl:*** Born **Birger Magnusson** (c. 1210) was a Swedish statesman, who played a pivotal role in the consolidation of Sweden. In 1250 he founded Stockholm. Several historical structures in Stockholm are named after him.

Burger Jarl

11

Stockholm's nucleus: the old town Gamla Stan was built between 1300 and 1500. Was a major Baltic trader which allowed it to develop strong economic and cultural linkages with many other European cities.

The Kalmar Union (1397–1523): A personal unions* that united the three kingdoms of Denmark, Norway (with Iceland, Greenland, Faroe Islands, Shetland, and Orkney) and Sweden (including part of Finland) under a single monarch.

> ***Personal Union:** An integration of several states under the same monarch while their laws, borders, and interests remain separate.

In 1520 uprising against the union and it's Danish King Christian II. The Danish king conquered the city and on November 8, 1520, conducted massive executions of opposition figures (the Stockholm Bloodbath). Further uprisings took place, which eventually led to the break-up of the Kalmar Union.

In 1523 Gustav Vasa* became the king of Sweden leading the Swedish War of Liberation from the Kalmar Union and the establishment of royal power. By 1600, the Stockholm population reached ten thousand.

***Gustav Eriksson** of the Vasa noble family known as **Gustav Vasa** (12 May 1496 – 29 Sep 1560), was King of Sweden from 1523 until his death in 1560 He ended the Kalmar Union and initiated the hereditary monarchy under the House of Vasa and its successors.

Gustav Vasa

17th century Sweden became a major European power: 1610 to 1680 population growth six-fold, 1634 Stockholm became the capital of the Swedish empire, the city monopolized trade between foreigners, Swedish & Scandinavians

The Great Northern War (1700-1721): Russia, Denmark-Norway, Poland-Lithuania & Saxony engaged Sweden for supremacy in the Baltic Sea. Sweden was defeated. Russia became the new major power in the Baltic Sea. 1710 the Black Death reached the city.

1721 The end of the **Great Northern War**: Sweden defeated, Stockholm stagnated, population growth halted, economic growth slowed. However, the city maintained its role as Sweden's political center.

The Bounce Back (2nd half of the 19th century): Stockholm regained its leading economic role. New industries emerged, transformed the city into a major trade center. The population grew through immigration. By the end of the century, scientific institutes opened.

20th – 21st Centuries: Stockholm became a modern, technologically-advanced & ethnically diverse city. Many industries were shifted into high-technology and service-related. The city Architects inspired by Berlin & Vienna.

Population: Population of ~2 million (48% of residents are of minority heritage). Languages spoken are Swedish, English, Arabic, Turkish, Kurdish, Finnish, Persian, Spanish & Serbian.

Geography: Located on the south-central east coast of Sweden. Built on 14 islands and islets in Lake Malaren. Lake Mälaren meets the Baltic Sea. The Geographical city center is situated on the water.

The 14 Islands & islets are:

- 1.   Beckholmen
- 2.   Djurgården - Nordic & Vasaa museum
- 3.   Helgeandsholmen – The Parliament
- 4.   Kastellholmen
- 5.   Kungsholmen
- 6.   Lilla Essingen
- 7.   Långholmen
- 8.   Reimersholmen
- 9.   Riddarholmen – Gamla Stan
- 10. Skeppsholmen – military museum
- 11. Stadsholmen - Gamla stan
- 12. Stora Essingen
- 13. Strömsborg – Gamla Stan
- 14. Södermalm

Tourism: Important to the economy. From 1991–2018 annual overnight stays increased from 4 million to over 9 million.

International Ranking:

- The best Marathon in the world
- The most innovative city in Europe
- The most competitive outside the USA
- Greenest & most livable city in the world
- Strongest Scandinavian GDP

- Best Nordic city to locate a business

Economy: 85% of jobs are in service industries, no heavy industry makes the city very clean. Most jobs created are in high technology Corp. Largest employers: IBM, Ericsson, & Electrolux

Tourist attractions:

- The old town Gamla Stan

- Vasaa Museum where the world's best-preserved ship of the era is housed

- Nordic Museum displays Swedish history from the 16th century

- City Hall Where the Nobel Prizes are awarded

- Stockholm Palace, the official residence of the Swedish King

- The Royal Armory, within the Stockholm Palace

- Ericsson Globe, the model of the Sun and the center of the model of the solar system

Gamla Stan
(The Old City)

The Vasa (A 1628 Warship): Sank in the harbor during its maiden voyage in 110 ft of water & 20 min from launching point. Discovered in1956 and brought to the surface, restored and housed in its own museum. It is the world's best-preserved warship of its kind. It is loaded with guns on 2 levels even though it was designed for only one level of guns (that what happen when politicians interfere in technology, the ship sink). Out of the hundreds and possibly thousands of similar ships built throughout the world, this is the only one survived because it sunk. This museum is located next to the Nordic museum.

The Vasaa Museum

The Nordic Museum: Located next to the Vasa museum. The museum displays the Swedish culture from the 16th century to the present day.

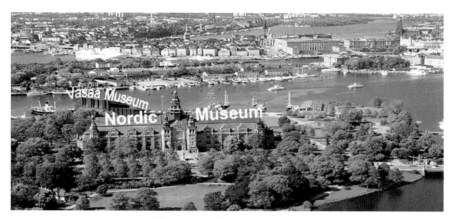

The Nordic Museum

The City Hall: Where the Nobel Prizes are awarded

Stockholm Palace: The official residence of the Swedish King

The Royal Armory: Located within the Stockholm Palace

The Royal Armory

Ericsson Globe: the model of the Sun and the center of the model of the solar system

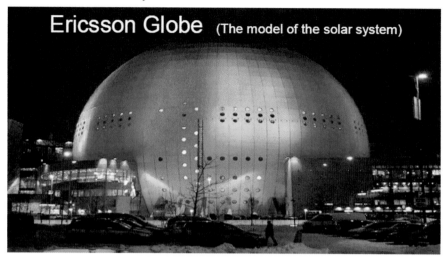

Ericson Globe

Cruise Ship Ports: Cruise ships can dock in two port areas as indicated on the map. If your ship dock in the northern port, Nordic and Vasa Museums are within 30-45 min walk, you need transportation to other attractions. If your ship dock in the southern port, Gamla Stan, Royal Palace and Armory and possibly the City Hall are within 30-45 min. walk, you need transportation to other attractions.

Location of Attractions

Cruise ships entrance to Stockholm: One of the world's longest and most scenic combinations of water and numerous occupied and undeveloped islands. If you miss the entrance don't worry, the exit will be the same way in the opposite direction.

Currency:

- The krona since 1873

- 1 Swedish Krona = ~0.11$US

Climate:

- Humid continental climate

- Daylight varies widely

- 18+ hours summer to ~ 6 hours winter

- Mild temperatures & sunnier weather

- 45%+ days of sunshine annually

Climate Data for Stockholm

Month	Jan	Feb	Mar	Apr	May	Jun	Jul	Aug	Sep	Oct	Nov	Dec
Average high °C (°F)	-0.7 (31)	-0.6 (31)	3.0 (37)	8.6 (47)	15.7 (60)	20.7 (69)	21.9 (71)	20.4 (69)	15.1 (59)	9.9 (50)	4.5 (40)	1.1 (34)
Average low °C (°F)	-5 (23)	-5.3 (23)	-2.7 (27)	1.1 (34)	6.3 (43)	11.3 (52)	13.4 (56)	12.7 (54)	9.0 (48)	5.3 (42)	0.7 (33)	-3.2 (26)
Precip. mm (inches)	39 (1.5)	27 (1.1)	26 (1.0)	30 (1.2)	30 (1.2)	45 (1.8)	72 (2.8)	66 (2.6)	55 (2.2)	50 (2.0)	53 (2.1)	46 (1.8)

Tallinn, Estonia

Tallinn: Estonia's Capital and its largest city. Tallinn's old town is a United Nation Educational, Scientific and Cultural Organization (UNESCO)'s World Heritage Site*

> *A World Heritage Site is a place listed by UNESCO as of special cultural or physical significance. Catalogs & conserves sites of outstanding cultural, physical or natural importance to the common heritage of humanity

Tallinn is ranked a global City**

> **Global City: Important node in the global economic system due to geography & urban studies creating finance & trade globalization.

Tallinn is listed among the world's top Digital Cities***

> ***Digital City: Connected community through broadband communications infrastructure and Innovative services to meet the needs of governments & industries

In 2011 Tallinn was a European Capital of Culture: Designated by the European Union.

The Name:

Historical Placement: 1154 a Moroccan Cartographer, Al-Idrisi* placed a town called Qalaven on the world map. Some historians believe this is where Tallinn is today.

Almoravids: A Berber dynasty of Morocco formed an empire in the 11th century that stretched over northwest Africa and Iberia. Their capital was Marrakesh

*Muhammad Al-Idrisi (1100-1165): A Muslim geo-grapher, cartographer & Egyptologist Lived in Palermo, Sicily. Was born in Ceuta, Morocco.

Muhammad al-Idrisi

Synopsis of History:

First Human settlement: Found in the city center ~5000 yrs old ceramic pottery dates to around 3000 BC.

Historical Names: Reval was Tallinn German name 13th century until 1917 and 1941 to 1944 during Nazi occupation of Estonia. The seal below is Reval's in 1340

Strategic Location: 13th century the city was an important strategic location for trade between Russia & Scandinavia. This made the city a target for Denmark. By 1219 Denmark ruled the city.

German Connection: 1346 the Danes sold Reval to the Teutonic Knights*. Tallinn population was 8,000. The Knights fortified the city with walls and 66 defense towers.

*The Teutonic Knights: The Order of Brothers of the German House of Saint Mary in Jerusalem, A German medieval military order, was formed in 1190 in Acre, the Crusaders Kingdom of Jerusalem, to aid Christians on their pilgrimages to the Holy Land (Modern times a purely religious Catholic order).

Plague and Occupation: During the Great Northern War (1710-1721): Russia, Denmark-Norway, Poland-Lithuania & Saxony vs. Sweden. Plague-struck Tallinn & Estonia. 1710 Estonia capitulated to Imperial Russia

19th Century: the city and port industrialized. By 1890s Russification became stronger. Russia occupied Estonia.

Independence: 24 Feb 1918, Reval was renamed Tallinn. 2 Feb 1920, Russia acknowledged the independence of the Estonian Republic. Tallinn became the capital.

World War II: 1940 Estonia was annexed by the Union of Soviet Socialist Republic (USSR). 1941-1944 occupied by Nazi Germany. 1944 after the Nazi retreat was again annexed by the USSR. Tallinn became the capital of the Estonian Soviet Socialist Republic (SSR).

Modern Estonia: 20 Aug 1991 an independent democratic Estonian state was re-established again. Was quickly developed. Tallinn became a modern European capital

Tallinn Historical 3 Parts:

1. The Toompea or "Cathedral Hill". The seat of the central authority throughout its history

2. The Old Town, the "city of the citizens"

3. A crescent to the south of the Old Town, where the Estonians came to settle

Origin of Modern Name: Tallinn is derived from Tallide-linn (the City of Stables) or Taani-linn (Danish-castle/town) or Tali-linna (winter-castle/town) or Talu-linna (house/farmstead-castle/town).

Population: Population around 470K, 33% of Estonia's population lives in Tallinn

Ethnic Composition (2018)

Ethnic group	Percentage
Estonians	55%
Russians	36%
Ukrainians	4%
Belarusians	2%
Finns	1%
Others	2%

Languages: Official language is Estonian followed closely by Russian. Other languages include Ukrainian, Belarusian & Finnish.

Geography: Located on the southern coast of the Gulf of Finland, in north-western Estonia. East is Russia; south is Latvia; southwest and west is the Baltic Sea.

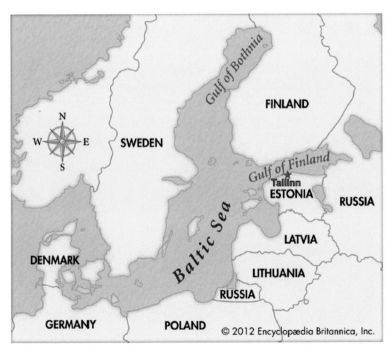

Currency: The Euro

Economy: The financial & business capital of Estonia. High level of economic freedom. Highly diversified economy. Strengths in information technology & tourism.

> **GDP:** Over ½ of the Estonian GDP is created in Tallinn. Tallinn GDP per capita is 172% of the Estonian average; 115% of the European Union (EU) average. Estonia GDP is 67% of the EU average.

Tourist Attractions: About 1.7 million visitors annually. Old Town, a UNESCO World Heritage Site Maritime Museum, Zoo & Open Air Museum. ~520,000 cruise ship passengers/year.

> **Toompea:** A limestone hill in the central part of the city, approximately 20–30 m. (62-93 ft) higher than the surrounding areas. Today Toompea is the center of the Estonian Government & Parliament and it is a UNESCO World Heritage Site.

Toompea Castle: In use since the 9th century. The Castle today houses the Parliament of Estonia

Stenbock House: on Toompea hill, the official seat of the Government of Estonia.

St. Mary's Cathedral (The Dome Church): Established by Danes in the 13th century. The oldest church in Tallinn. Originally a Roman Catholic cathedral, by 1561 became Lutheran. Today, the church belongs to the Estonian Evangelical Lutheran.

St. Olaf's Church

The World's Tallest Bldg?: 15th century a new 159 m (522 ft) high Gothic spire was built for St. Olaf's Church. Until 1625 it was the world's tallest building. After several fires and following rebuilding, today its overall height is 123 m (404 ft)

St. Nicholas' Church: a medieval church dedicated to St. Nicholas: was built in the 13th century, partially destroyed in Soviet Bombing of Tallinn in World War II. The church has been restored; today houses a branch of the Art Museum of Estonia.

Alexander Nevsky Cathedral: Orthodox cathedral in the Tallinn Old Town. Built from 1894-1900 in a typical Russian Revival style. Estonia was part of the Russian Empire.

Lower Town: One of Europe's best preserved medieval towns.

Major sights: the Town Hall square; the city wall and towers; Fat Margaret; medieval churches.

31

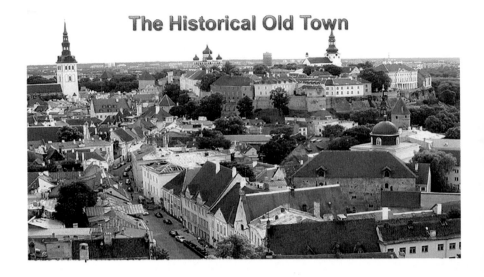

City Symbol: 1530 A weather vanes, the figure of a warrior called Old Thomas, was placed on top of the spire of the Town Hall became the symbol for the city.

City Wall

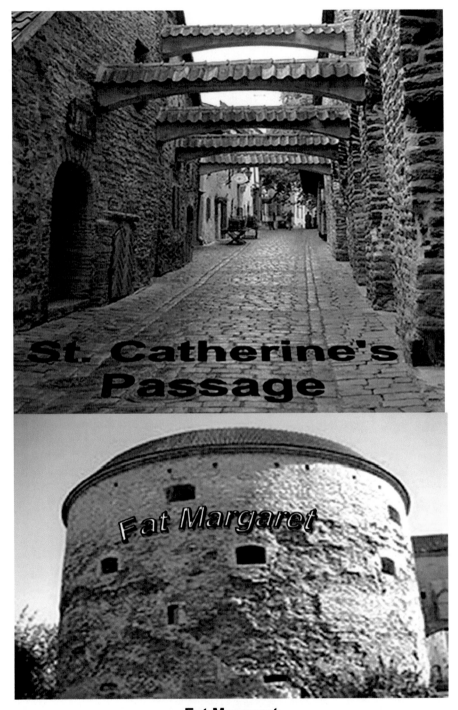

Fat Margaret

The cruise ship port: Located within walking distance from old town where most tourist attractions are (20 min walk), Toompea (30 min walk).

Location of Attractions Relative to Port

Climate Data for Tallinn

Month	Jan	Feb	Mar	Apr	May	Jun	Jul	Aug	Sep	Oct	Nov	Dec
Rec. high °C (°F)	9.2 (-49)	10.2 (50)	15.9 (61)	27.2 (81)	29.7 (86)	31.2 (88)	32.3 (90)	31.2 (88)	28.5 (83)	21.8 (71)	13.4 (56)	10.7 (51)
Ave. high °C (°F)	-2.9 (27)	-3 (27)	0.8 (33)	7.3 (45)	14.0 (57)	18.8 (66)	21.8 (71)	19.9 (68)	14.9 (59)	9.0 (48)	3.3 (38)	-0.2 (32)
Ave. low °C (°F)	-8.2 (17)	-8 (18)	-5.6 (22)	-0.2 (32)	4.9 (41)	9.9 (50)	12.5 (55)	12.0 (54)	8.0 (46)	3.7 (39)	-0.9 (30)	-4.9 (23)
Rec. low °C (°F)	-31.4 (-24)	-31 (-24)	-26.2 (-15)	-17.2 (1.0)	-4.3 (24)	0.0 (32)	4.4 (40)	1.7 (35)	-4.7 (24)	-10.5 (13)	-21.3 (-6)	-32.2 (-26)
Precip. mm (inches)	45 (1.8)	29 (1.1)	29 (1.1)	36 (1.4)	37 (1.5)	53 (2.1)	79 (3.1)	84 (3.3)	82 (3.2)	70 (2.8)	68 (2.7)	55 (2.2)

St. Petersburg, Russia

St. Petersburg: Russia's capital for 186 years.

The name: Peter the Great named the city after his patron saint (St. Peter).The name sound like Dutch. Peter's was obsessed with Dutch culture.

Peter I the Great Emperor of Russia

Synopsis of History: 1703 (during the Great Northern War 1700-1721)* Peter the Great captured the Swedish fortress of Nyenschantz; laid down Peter & Paul Fortress, Became the first building of the new city.

An abbreviated chronology of historical significance actions and associated emperors and other personnel are given below:

> ***The Great Northern War** (1700-1721): Russia, Denmark-Norway, Poland-Lithuania & Saxony coordinated attack on Sweden. 1721 Sweden defeated: Russia became the major power in the Baltic Sea under Peter the Great.

Peter
& Paul
Fortress
(Zayachy
Island)

Peter and Paul Cathedral

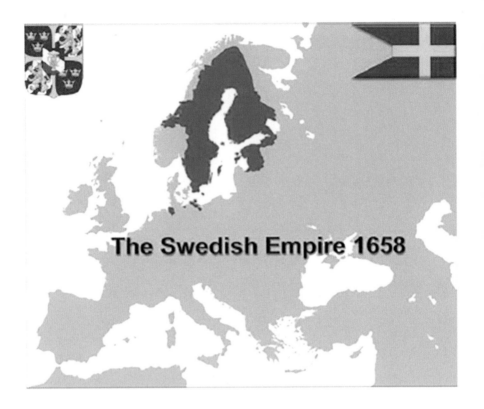

The Swedish Empire 1658

The Capital: 1712 Peter the Great Moved the capital from Moscow to St. Petersburg; 1721 ended the Great Northern War & annexed the territory. Hired Domenici Trezzini* as the fort (Peter and Paul Fort) and city architect.

*Domenici Trezzini (1670-1734) (A Swiss-Italian Architect):

Elaborated the Petrine Baroque style of Russian architecture

His son had Peter I as a godfather

Designed Peter and Paul Cathedral

1716 Designed St. Petersburg city center.

Serfdom: A condition of bondage/modified slavery developed during the middle ages in Europe, including Russia. Application of serfdom resulted in enforced labor by landowners in return for protection & the right to work. 1000s of serfs died building the city.

The Price of Progress: Peter the Great push for modernization met with opposition from nobility resulting in several attempts on his life. One of the treason cases involved his own son.

Peterhof "Russian Versailles" (UNESCO World Heritage Site): laid out on the orders of Peter the Great on the south shore of the Gulf of Finland. Currently, hosts 1 of 2 campuses of St Petersburg University. Peterhof consists of a series of palaces and gardens.

Peterhof Palace

Peter II of Russia (Emperor 1725-1730): The only son of Peter I. 1725 Peter the Great died. Peter II became the emperor. 1728, moved his seat back to Moscow. 1730 Peter II died.

Anna Ivanovna (Empress 1730-1740): Government dominated by German advisers. 1732 St Petersburg again became the capital of the Russian Empire; remained the capital for the next 186 years.

Catastrophic Fire (1736): Destroyed most of the city. 1737 Burkhard Christoph von Münnich* oversaw a city plan to rebuild the city.

> ***Count Von Münnich:** Served in the French & Polish-Saxon armies; 1721 entered the service of Peter I; 1728 Peter II gave him the title of count & was appointed Commander in Chief of the Russian Army; 1732 Made a field marshal & president of the war council.

Empress Elizabeth (Empress 1740-1760): No German allowed in the government. The City became a fine European capital to rival those in the West. She was fluent in Italian, German & French. She was the most popular ruler. She ordered the reconstruction of **Catherine Palace**.

Catherine Palace: Used as headquarter for the German Army in WW II and was mostly destroyed and rebuilt after the war. After the war, the Russian discovered that the palace's **Amber Room** was missing and has not been recovered. The current Amber room was constructed after WWII.

The Amber Room: Completely lined with amber (must see)

The Amber Room (Catherine Palace)

Catherine the Great (Empress 1760-1796): Founded the **Hermitage Museum**; bought vast amount of art from Europe (over 3 million items); lined the banks of the Neva River with granite embankments; commissioned the **Bronze Horseman** (statue of Peter the Great); ordered that no structure be higher than the **Winter Palace**; prohibited  spacing between buildings; no permanent bridges across the Neva River (only pontoon bridges allowed).

The Hermitage Museum consists of 5 buildings: Hermitage Theater, Old Hermitage, New Hermitage, Small Hermitage, and the Winter Palace. Half of the General staff building also belongs to the Hermitage Museum. The other half is used by the Western Military District of Russia.

General Staff Building

Hermitage Theater   Old Hermitage   New Hermitage   Small Hermitage   Winter Palace

Changes in Architect & Decors: Baroque & Rococo styles dominated for 60 years (Winter Palace & Catherine Palace...) 1760s **Neoclassical** is a new style.

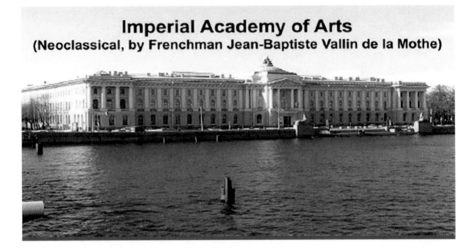

Emperor Paul (Emperor 1796-1801): was overshadowed by his mother until he was assassinated in 1801.

Alexander I (Emperor 1801-1825): He was victorious over Napoleon's France in 1812. Alexander Column in the Palace Square commemorates this victory. The column is 47.5 m tall and topped with a statue of an angel holding a cross.

Nicholas I (Emperor 1825-1855): He was expansionist, under his rule the Russian Empire reached its geographical zenith, spanning over 20 million square kilometers (7.7 million square miles).

Alexander II (Emperor 1855-1881): St. Petersburg surpassed Moscow in population and industrial growth and became one of the largest cities in Europe. He abolished Serfdom and elevated Finland language in Finland to the same level as the Swedish (see Alexander II statue in Senate Square, Helsinki, Finland in this book).

More Architectural Changes (1840-1890): Neoclassical to **Romanticist** styles. Examples: Marlinsky and Beloselsky-Belozersky Palaces, Moskovsky Rail Terminal and the Church of the Savior on Blood.

Moskovsky Rail Terminal

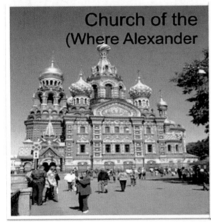

Church of the Savior on Blood
(Where Alexander II was Assassinated)

1881-1894, Alexander III followed by Nicholas II (1894-1917)

St. Petersburg to Petrograd: 1905 revolution began in St. Petersburg. 100s of demonstrators shot in front of the Winter Palace. At the start of World War I, the name was perceived to be too German; by 1914, the city was renamed Petrograd.

The Revolution: Two revolutions were required in order to change the composition of Russia:

-1917, February Revolution, appeared to break out spontaneously and resulted in the Tsar overthrow.

-1917, October Revolution, bringing Bolshevik rule and a change in Russia's social structure paving the way for the Union of the Soviet Socialist Republic (USSR).

Capital to Moscow: 1918 Lenin* transferred the capital to Moscow. Petrograd Was too close to the border and anti-Soviet foreign armies.

> *Vladimir Lenin was a Russian revolutionary politician. He served as head of government of Soviet Russia from 1917 to 1924.

Red Terror: 1917-1920, many people fled the city due to civil war and repression in the Red Terror. The population of the city decreased dramatically.

Petrograd to Leningrad: 1924, 3 days after Lenin death, Petrograd was renamed Leningrad.

The Cruiser Aurora (Аврóра): Her crew joined the 1917 Revolution. On 25 Oct 1917, a blank shot from her gun signaled the start of the assault on the Winter Palace which was the beginning of the October Revolution. For decades after the

The Cruiser Aurora (Аврóра) (A Museum)

revolution, Leningrad was glorified as "The Cradle of the revolution".

Stalinist Architectures: 1935 a new plan for the city was outlined included the new Stalinist architectures.

World War II: Leningrad was besieged by Nazi Germany for 872 days (8 Sep 1941 to 27 Jan 1944). The longest, most destructive and lethal sieges of major cities in modern history. The siege isolated the Leningrad from most supplies and as a result, more than one million civilians died, mostly from starvation, and the city became largely depopulated.

Broken Ring Monument: Signify the city successful battle to lift the Nazi siege of Leningrad.

WW II, 1941 monument

Post World War II: The city was rebuilt partially according to the pre-war plans. The Leningrad metro opened in 1955.

Leningrad Metro

After the Death of Stalin: The Stalinist architectures were abandoned. By 1960s through the 1980s new residential boroughs built consist of functionalist apartment blocks identical to each other. These apartments allow families to move in from communal apartments in the city center.

Democracy: June 12, 1991, 54% of voters chose to restore the name Saint Petersburg to the city. Many other Soviet-era landmarks renamed.

Population of Saint Petersburg

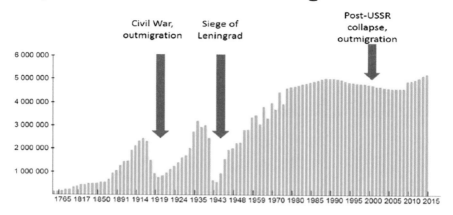

Museums: The city is home to more than 200 museums most are hosted in historic buildings. The largest of the museums is the Hermitage Museum featuring the Imperial residence and their vast art collection.

City's Architects: The architect of the city center mostly Baroque and Neoclassical buildings of the 18th and 19th centuries largely preserved. The historic city center and related monument are UNESCO World Heritage Sites

The uniqueness of St. Petersburg: Well preserved castles, museums, monuments and sculptures, long straight boulevards, vast spaces, gardens and parks, decorative fences, the Neva River and its many canals, granite embankments and bridges.

Tourism: Foreign visitors need a visa to enter the country. Cruise ship passengers, however, need a visa only if they want to wander on their own. Ship tours include the required visa. If you want to be on your own then take a cheap shopping tour or St. Petersburg on your own tour and then utilize local taxis and transportations to visit the sites. I highly recommend that you take ship tours to visit the Hermitage Museum, Catherine Palace, Peter and Paul Fortress and Peterhof (see map). Catherine Palace and Peterhof are about 25 km each from the ship dock. Most of the other sites are within the city (relatively short distances from each other).

Must see: The Hermitage/Winter Palace/museum, Peter and Paul Fortress, and Peter and Paul Cathedral, Catherine Palace, Peterhof, Church of the Savior on Blood, the Bronze Horseman and Russia Museum.

The 2 maps below indicate the location of the recommended tourist sites.

Location of Attractions

St. Isaac Cathedral

Kazan Cathedral

Climate Data for St. Petersburg

Month	Jan	Feb	Mar	Apr	May	Jun	Jul	Aug	Sep	Oct	Nov	Dec
Rec. High °C (°F)	8.3 (47)	10.2 (50)	14.9 (59)	25.3 (78)	30.9 (88)	.34.6 (94)	35.3 (96)	37.1 (99)	30.4 (87)	21.0 (70)	12.3 (54)	10.9 (52)
Ave. High °C (°F)	-3.1 (26)	-3 (27)	2.0 (36)	9.3 (49)	16.0 (61)	20.0 (68)	23.0 (73)	20.8 (69)	15.0 (59)	8.6 (48)	2.0 (36)	-1.5 (29)
Ave. Low °C (°F)	-8 (18)	-8.5 (17)	-4.2 (24)	1.5 (35)	7.0 (45)	11.7 (53)	15.0 (59)	13.5 (56)	8.8 (48)	4.0 (39)	-1.8 (29)	-6.1 (21)
Rec. Low °C (°F)	-35.9 (-33)	-35.2 (-31)	-29.9 (-22)	-21.8 (-7)	-6.6 (20)	0.1 (32)	4.9 (41)	1.3 (34)	-3.1 (26)	-12.9 (9)	-22.2 (-8)	-34.4 (-30)
Ave. Precip. mm (inches)	44 (1.7)	33 (1.3)	37 (1.5)	31 (1.2)	46 (1.8)	71 (2.8)	79 (3.1)	83 (3.3)	64 (2.5)	68 (2.7)	55 (2.2)	51 (2)

Helsinki, Finland

Helsinki: Finland's capital & largest city.

The name: Early settlers were Swedish. By 1548 established new town called Helsinge Fors, (the Helsinge Rapids). This name then evolved into Helsingfors, Today is the name of the city in Swedish. This evolved into Helsinki.

Synopsis of History:1249-1650 Swedish era occupation. 1550 Sweden established it as a trading town to rival Rival (today Tallinn). Helsinki remained a poor tiny town. 1696-97 (during the Little Ice Age*) suffered a severe famine, $1/3^{rd}$ of the population died. 1710 The plague killed 50% of inhabitants. 1714-1721** and 1741-1743*** Russia occupied Helsinki. 1808 fire destroyed 1/4ter of Helsinki. Summer 1866 extreme rain resulted in crops failure, stored food ran out. 1867 summer temp 8°C below normal, rivers & lakes remained frozen until June. Harvest was 1/2 the average, 15% of the population died. 1809-1917, Finland became an autonomous region in the Russian Empire. 1812, Czar Alexander I of Russia moved the Finnish capital from Turku to Helsinki, bringing the capital closer to St. Petersburg, Russia's capital. The Finnish language gained recognition during Alexander II of Russia. 1906, Strong desire for independence. 1917 The Finnish Parliament declared independence. This led to civil war (thousands died); pro-independence won. 1919, Finland was declared a republic.

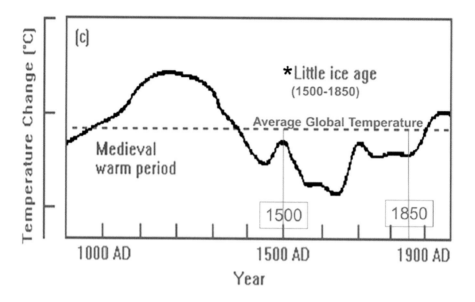

**The Great Northern War (1700-1721): Russia, Denmark-Norway, Poland-Lithuania & Saxony coordinated attack on Sweden. 1721 Sweden was defeated: Russia became the major power in the Baltic Sea under Peter the Great.

***The Lesser Wrath war (1741-1743) Between Sweden and Russia: Russia occupied Finland.

Modern history: 1939 USSR-Germany pact (Molotov–Ribbentrop Pact) enabled USSR to invade Lithuania, Latvia, Estonia, and Finland without German interference. The 3 Baltic countries gave in to Soviet demands, Finland refused. 30 November 1939, USSR attacked Finland. 12 Mar 1940, Finland avoided annexation by signing the treaty ending the war. Finland lost to USSR 20% of the country's industry 11% of agricultural land, Viipuri, second largest city. 1941-1944 Finland army helped Germany in the battle of Leningrad (St. Petersburg). 1947 & 48 treaties signed with the Soviet Union, Finland lost 10% of its land & 20% of its industrial capacity. 400,000 evacuees fled these areas. Finland remained neutral during the cold war (1948-

1990). 1952 hosted the XV Olympic Games. 1995 joined the European Union. 2011, the Monocle Magazine ranked Helsinki the most livable city in the world in its Livable Cities Index.

Population: approximately 630K; the metropolitan population of ~1.5 million, the most populous urban area in Finland. Helsinki is the world's northernmost metro area of over one million people. The northernmost capital of a European Union member state; the third largest city in the Nordic nations after Copenhagen & Stockholm.

Geography: Located on the shore of the Gulf of Finland, 80 km (50 mi) north of Tallinn, 400 km (250 mi) east northeast of Stockholm, 300 km (190 mi) West of Saint Petersburg. The city has close historical connections with all these cities.

Tourism: About 3.1 million foreign tourists per year visit Finland, most to Helsinki.

Attractions: Below is major tourist sites and their locations.

Helsinki Metro

– Helsinki University

Helsinki University

– **Temppeliaukio Church (The Rock Church):** A Lutheran church opened in 1969, built directly into the solid rock.

The Rock Church

Sibelius Monument

Helsinki Evangelical Lutheran Cathedral fronted by a statue of Emperor Alexander II of Russia: Built 1830-1852. Alexander II was the Emperor of Russia from 2 March 1855 until his assassination on 13 March 1881. He elevated the Finnish language to the same level as the Swedish's. The Finnish erected his statue here as an appreciation of this act.

Helsinki Cathedral

Uspenski Orthodox Cathedral

Kaippatri Market Square

Attractions Map: Showing the location of the above point of interest. If you are a good walker, you can reach most of these points by walking from the cruise ship port or Helsinki port. You can also ride the Hop on Hop off to these places.

Location of Attractions

Climate data for Helsinki

Month	Jan	Feb	Mar	Apr	May	Jun	Jul	Aug	Sep	Oct	Nov	Dec
Rec. high °C (°F)	8.5 (47)	11.8 (53)	15.1 (59)	21.9 (71)	27.6 (82)	30.9 (88)	34.0 (93)	31.2 (88)	26.2 (79)	17.5 (64)	11.6 (53)	10.0 (50)
Ave. high °C (°F)	-1.3 (30)	-1.9 (29)	1.6 (35)	7.6 (46)	14.4 (58)	18.5 (65)	21.5 (71)	19.8 (68)	14.6 (58)	9.0 (48)	3.7 (39)	0.5 (33)
Ave. low °C (°F)	-6.5 (20)	-7.4 (19)	-4.1 (25)	0.8 (33)	6.3 (43)	10.9 (52)	14.2 (58)	13.1 (56)	8.7 (48)	4.3 (40)	-0.6 (31)	-4.5 (24)
Rec. low °C (°F)	-34.3 (-30)	-31.5 (-25)	-24.5 (-12)	-16.3 (3)	-4.8 (23)	0.7 (33)	5.4 (42)	2.8 (37)	-4.5 (24)	-11.6 (11)	-18.6 (-2)	-29.5 (-21)
Precip. mm (inches)	52 (2.1)	36 (1.4)	38 (1.5)	32 (1.3)	37 (1.5)	57 (2.2)	63 (2.5)	80 (3.2)	56 (2.2)	76 (3.0)	70 (2.8)	58 (2.3)

Copenhagen, Denmark

Copenhagen: Denmark's capital & largest city.

The name: Adaptation from Low German Copenhagen. A composite from Latin and German loosely meaning merchants/tradesman.

Synopsis of History: 11th century, first settlement. 12th-13th centuries Copenhagen expanded and was fortified with a stone wall and chartered as a city. By the end of the 16th century, other districts incorporated into Copenhagen making the city Denmark's principal port and center of Northern Europe trade.

In the17th and 18th century resisted difficult Swedish siege, repelled a major assault and was ravaged by large fires. The fires destroyed most of the medieval part of Copenhagen. At the beginning of the 19th century, the British navy bombarded Copenhagen as part of the Battle of Copenhagen using new long-range guns. These guns rendered the city old defenses useless. The city suffered extensive damage and hundreds of people were killed.

Modern history: By 1901 the city growth incorporated Frederiksberg municipality as an enclave within Copenhagen. World War II, Copenhagen, and Denmark were occupied by German troops. After WWII, extensive infrastructures were built making the city very attractive for international business. In the year 2000, major international toll bridge/tunnel (Øresund Bridge) connected Copenhagen to the Swedish city of Malmo.

Population: Approximately 777,000 the most populous city of Denmark.

Geography: Copenhagen is located on the eastern shore of the island of Zealand and on a number of natural and artificial islets. East is the Øresund strait that separates Denmark from Sweden and connects the North Sea with the Baltic Sea. The Swedish towns of Malmö and Landskrona lie directly across the Øresund strait from Copenhagen.

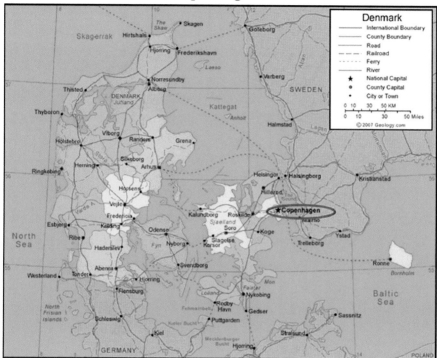

Tourism: Copenhagen is one of the fastest growing tourist destinations in Europe. Tourism contributed about $320 million. In addition, about 680,000 cruise passengers visit Copenhagen each year.

Copenhagen

67

Economy: The city is the major economic and financial center of Denmark. Most of its economy is based on services and commerce. The metro area GDP per capita is the 15th largest in the European Union.

Tourist attractions: **The port area**

Gefian Fountain

Tivoli Garden

Town Hall Square

Opera House   Amalienborg Palace

Change of the Guards at the Palace

Change of the Guard at the Palace

The Harbor

Christiansborg Palace

The Øresund Bridge-Tunnel

The Øresund Bridge-Tunnel

Location of Attractions

Climate data for Copenhagen

Month	Jan	Feb	Mar	Apr	May	Jun	Jul	Aug	Sep	Oct	Nov	Dec
Ave. high °C (°F)	1.9 (35)	2.0 (36)	4.8 (41)	9.5 (49)	15.0 (59)	19.2 (67)	20.4 (69)	20.3 (69)	16.7 (62)	12.1 (54)	7.1 (45)	3.7 (39)
Ave. low °C (°F)	-2 (28)	-2.4 (28)	-0.6 (31)	2.3 (36)	7.2 (45)	11.3 (52)	12.9 (55)	12.6 (55)	9.8 (52)	6.7 (44)	2.7 (37)	-0.5 (31)
Precip. mm (inches)	46 (1.8)	30 (1.2)	39 (1.5)	39 (1.5)	42 (1.7)	52 (2.1)	68 (2.7)	64 (2.5)	60 (2.4)	56 (2.2)	61 (2.4)	56 (2.2)

Made in the USA
Middletown, DE
05 March 2020